Pet Friends!

by Steve Hatch
illustrated by Fernando Luiz

Harcourt
SCHOOL PUBLISHERS

Requests for permission to make copies of any part of the work should be addressed to School Permissions and Copyrights, Harcourt, Inc., 6277 Sea Harbor Drive, Orlando, Florida 32887-6777. Fax: 407-345-2418.

HARCOURT and the Harcourt Logo are trademarks of Harcourt, Inc., registered in the United States of America and/or other jurisdictions.

Printed in China

ISBN 10: 0-15-350492-7
ISBN 13: 978-0-15-350492-1

Ordering Options
ISBN 10: 0-15-350333-5 (Grade 3 Below-Level Collection)
ISBN 13: 978-0-15-350333-7 (Grade 3 Below-Level Collection)
ISBN 10: 0-15-357478-X (package of 5)
ISBN 13: 978-0-15-357478-8 (package of 5)

2 3 4 5 6 7 8 9 10 985 12 11 10 09 08 07

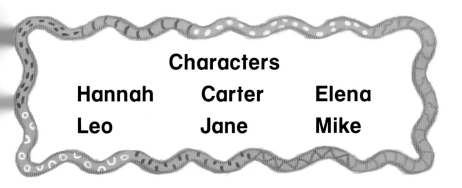

Setting: The offices of *Pet Friends* magazine

Hannah: Good morning! Let's work on the advice page for our next issue.

Carter: Plenty of letters arrived this month. I have taken a glimpse at some of them. They seemed really interesting.

Elena: So many kids want to consult us with questions about pets.

Hannah: It's very encouraging. They must think we give sensible advice!

Leo: Here's a brief letter to start:

Dear *Pet Friends*,

    Does my cat need a bath?

Yours,

Clean Cat

Mike: What do you think, Leo?

Leo: My answer is pretty good, I think.

Dear Clean,

Cats usually don't need baths. However, brushing gets rid of loose hair and dirt. Start by brushing for just a few minutes. Soon your cat will get used to it. Many cats even like it!

Cats may need a bath if they get into something dirty or sticky. If that happens, ask your vet or the people at your pet shop for advice on cat baths!

Best Wishes,

Leo

Pet Friends Cat Expert

Elena: Great answer, Leo! Here's my question:

Dear *Pet Friends*,

My family is going on a trip. I want to take our bird, Flutter. My mother says Flutter will be bothersome. He could cause a din in the car that might disturb the driver. What do you think?

Sincerely,

Flutter Fan

Jane: I sobbed when I left my dog with my grandmother during our vacation! What do you recommend, Elena?

Elena: Listen:

Dear Flutter,

Birds can travel! Bringing enough food and water is important. Putting a towel over the cage will calm Flutter and keep her from rustling around.

However, vacations can be very busy. Will you have enough time for Flutter? Your bird may be happier at home with a bird sitter than in a strange hotel room. Good luck!
Elena
Pet Friends Bird Expert

Mike: Listen to this letter:

Dear *Pet Friends*,
    We just got a rabbit! Her name is Pineapple. She's great! She chews on things around the house, though. What should I do?
Your friend,
Bunny Buddy

Leo: Is that unusual, Mike?

Mike: No, it's not. My answer explains what to do.

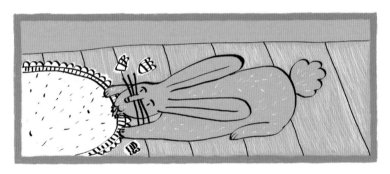

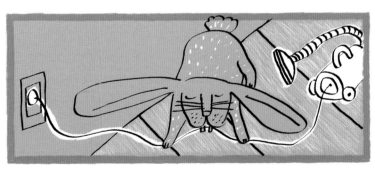

Dear Bunny,

   Rabbits chew a lot! The best way to keep rabbits from chewing your things is to keep them busy with their own things.

   Devise a playground for Pineapple. Give her cardboard tubes, boxes, or paper bags. She will enjoy dodging around and through them. She also can chew on the cardboard. Good luck!

Mike

Pet Friends Rabbit Expert

Jane: That sounds like good advice!
Now listen to my letter:

Dear *Pet Friends*,
    Do fish have memories?
Sincerely,
Curious

Carter: Good question! Well, Jane?

Jane: Listen:

Dear Curious,
    Yes! Fish remember places with food.
They remember their nests. Fish know more
than we think! Thanks for asking!
Jane
Pet Friends Fish Expert

Hannah: I've always wondered that—now I know! Well, everyone, I suppose that's all we can fit into this issue. There's plenty more for next month, though!

Leo: I can't wait to get started!

Think Critically

1. What happens at the beginning of this Readers' Theater?

2. Why do you think the author wrote this Readers' Theater?

3. Do you think "Flutter Fan" will take the bird on the trip or not? Explain your answer.

4. How do you think the kids choose the questions they will answer?

5. Which question do you think is the most interesting? Why?

 Social Studies

Pet Place Map Look in a telephone directory to find places in your town that have to do with pets. Make a list of pet shops, veterinarians, and animal shelters. Add their addresses and phone numbers. Keep the list for yourself if you have a pet or give it to someone else who does.

 School-Home Connection Talk to family members about pets. Discuss whether they've had any pets. Ask what they liked best about having a pet.

Word Count: 514